Finding Career

Freedom:

60 Days to Increase Your Confidence, Make Boss Money, and Get Unstuck at Work

By: Ashley Dash, MBA, JCDC, JCTC

Table of Contents

Dedication

For my favorite Mommy Girl. Your love has carried me, your belief has lifted me, and your arms have comforted me. Our laughter knows no bounds, and neither does our support. This book is for you.

-Love,

Boot

Acknowledgements

To my OE&D Team who taught me to ALWAYS put my best foot forward and do what is right. You know who you are. I thank you, I appreciate you, and I love you.

To my FIA sisters and our Fearless Leader, without your explicit expectations this book would have never been happened. I appreciate you ladies and your honesty, feedback, and support.

To Seven Degrees of Sigma, your words have encouraged me, your faith has strengthened me, and your fun times have kept me rejuvenated even in my darkest hour.

To the Decatur Crew, your support and help has meant the world to me.

To my accountability partner and her husband, thanks for loaning her to me for the countless hours of brainstorming, feedback, and silliness!

And finally, to my god-parentals, thanks for feeding me, supporting me, and letting me interrupt your daily routine and lives when I crashed your home repeatedly.

In the literary genius of the late and great Tupac Shakur, "You are appreciated!".

Introduction

My superpower is asking questions.

I began reading at the age of three, and it really freaked my mom out. She wasn't prepared to deal with a reading 3-year-old and all the questions that came along with it. However, instead of squashing the curiosity out of me, she fed it with books, encyclopedias, trivia games, and more.

Today, it's a cultivated skill 25+ years in the making. My power in asking thought-provoking questions shapes how I elevate my clients. I can do the same for you if I'm ever honored with the opportunity. This guide gives you an intimate look at my skills, expectations, and how you too can enjoy career freedom.

- Enjoy!

Chapter 1: How Did I Get Here?

"Ashley, it's done." I couldn't believe it. With the stroke of a pen, I was now the owner of my very own investment property. No mortgage or mountain of paperwork to sign, just a wire transfer and the keys. Sheesh. I know I planned for this, but, what was I thinking?

Did I really just pour my burgeoning emergency fund into a rinky-dink place in South Carolina? At the time, I was living in New Jersey. Why did no one try to stop me? Can I really do this? Can I really make this work? I feel like I just jumped off a cliff without a helping hand to save me.

How did I end up here?

The resounding question above in addition to many others, and the deafening silence afterwards, has been a central theme throughout my life. How I make decisions typically goes a little something like this: I decide to do something (usually something pretty crazy). I get an unexpected result. Then I cry out loud, usually to God, "What did I just do?". Next, I ask myself, "How did I get here?" Finally, I rinse and repeat, because obviously, I'm a glutton for punishment.

It's the same cycle I went through in April of 2012, when a recruiter said to me, "Congratulations Ashley, we would like to make you an offer to come work at Mercedes-Benz." My initial thought was, "Hold the presses, what did you just say?".

Rinse and repeat. This time I applied for a job located roughly 662.5 miles away from home thinking that there isn't a chance I'd get hired. Here goes the unexpected result.

They fly me up first class to New Jersey for the interview. I'm in denial thinking they are just being nice, because in my mind they can't REALLY be serious.

I cry out loud and accept a temporary lateral project position in a different state and have to leave my family and friends.

Oh God, what did I just do.

Sobbing in my 2005 Honda Civic packed with my personal belongings as I see the "Welcome to New Jersey" sign flash across my windshield heading towards a very uncertain future, here I am again wondering how I got here. At this point it's too late to change my mind and return the relocation money.

I'm all in.

Looking back, I can laugh because my tears were unwarranted and definitely unnecessary. Yet, I didn't know that at the time. Initially, all I could see in front of me was what I was giving up. Things.

Very important things that I hac learned to love including:

- My townhouse that wasn't even three years old.
- The haven of my tight-knit family who always had my back.
- My safe circle of friends that I'd come to lean on for support.
- My newly adopted city of Charlotte, NC where culture, fun, and food could be found.

I had not yet had the opportunity to see what I was gaining. Thankfully, I can borrow a line from "A Tale of Two Cities," and say, "It was the best of times...." Working for Mercedes-Benz was one of the highlights of my career. The experiences, the people, the travel, and the cars are unmatched. When they say luxury automotive brand, they mean it. I felt like I'd entered a secret society for the well to-do who hobnob with the rich and famous. I'll never forget:

- Black Car service transfers to and fro with little signs with your name on them that made you feel like a true VIP.

- Chocolate covered strawberries and champagne meetings for birthday celebrations in the middle of the day.

- My daily subsidized breakfast consisting of a vegetable egg-white omelet with cheese, made to order at our onsite cafeteria (Thank-You Sodexo!).

- Free Mercedes-Benz car loans you could borrow for the weekend.
- Team-building exercises that included spa services.
- Offsite retreats at luxury mountain resorts with s'mores and tricycles we built for special needs children.
- Learning archery in the Black Forest of Germany while seafood was barbequed on an open fire (Yes, this is a thing, and it really happened!).

Working at Mercedes was AMAZING. Something I've only ever dreamed of, but never thought I'd experience in real life. In fact, I felt like I'd just stumbled into a scene from *The Devil Wears Prada* and was doing a really crummy job attempting to impersonate Anne Hathaway. I landed a role a million of girls would clamor for with all the cool perks to match.

Except instead of a lunatic micromanager of a boss, I got a manager sent from Heaven who became my mentor and helped guide my career. In fact, you can say she helped guide me to you, and every word you are reading right now. It was under her careful eye, that my training, development, and education all flourished.

She possessed every positive attribute you can ever wish for in a leader. She was honest, compassionate, genuine interested in you as a person, and she believed in professional and personal development. It was like I hit the million-dollar Powerball jackpot of mentors. And not only was my supervisor amazing, but so were my co-workers.

The stories, the laughter, and the trust are forever with me.

I finally understood what people meant when they said they were excited to get up in the morning and go to work. Finally, I felt appreciated, respected, and heard at work. For the first time, I didn't have to live paycheck-to-paycheck and I was able to save money, pay off credit card debt and help support my mom.

And that rinky-dink apartment was my investment present to myself. A sort of congratulatory memento of this time in my life. It became a saving grace, not just for me, but for members of my family. It became a place of safety, security, and an asset I could leverage for future entrepreneurial endeavors.

A reminder for me of a radical decision that changed my life. To this day, it is one of the best and scariest decisions I've ever made. A physical reminder that says, "You can't go wrong when you trust yourself, and invest in yourself personally or professionally."

Working at Mercedes-Benz, I became a homeowner, HR professional, and Real

Estate mogul in the making. Finally, I felt like I had arrived.

Chapter 2: What's Wrong with Me?

May 2008

"Thank you very much for your interest, but we have decided to go with another candidate who is a better match for the job requirements of the position. We appreciate you taking the time to apply for employment with our company and wish you the best of luck in your future endeavors."

Dang! Another rejection email. I started receiving them so frequently, I'd lost count. Another dream deferred. Another opportunity gone down the drain. However, there was a silver lining. After applying for so many jobs, I was just glad to get ANY communication back at all. I came to realize that all of my time and effort to fill out all those tiny, stupid boxes online after I submitted my resume, were not in vain. I was starting to think that somehow my job applications were getting stuck in some type of space-time continuum where resumes and cover letters went to die, never ever to be heard from again.

With my stomach growling, there was no need to check the fridge. Tonight's adventurous dinner option was that of Top Ramen. Hopefully, I had one more shrimp packet left because I was tired of chicken. I knew it was unhealthy, but at this point it was all I could afford.

Academic scholar, college graduate, multiple corporate internships; Ashley Dash was reduced to eating Ramen Noodles without a job prospect in sight. And with student loan payments looming in the very near future, the glow from graduation day last December was becoming an increasingly distant memory. It was times like these, when one asked thoughtful, insightful, soul-searching questions such as, "Am I being punked?". Where was Ashton Kutcher when you needed him? This certainly could not be the story of my life.

You see, I did everything "they" told me to do, so I could get a "good job," and not move back home to the abyss of

Jackson, South Carolina. They, known as college professors and peers, said:

1. Go to college. Hello Winthrop University!
2. Choose the right major. Can't go wrong with a degree in Business.
3. Update your resume.
4. Network with your alumni.
5. Get some good work experience.
6. Don't wait until the last minute to find a job. I started applying for jobs six months before graduation!
7. Remember to save and build your emergency fund.

Got it!

So, after listening to all of the advice, and going on countless interviews, why was I on the verge of being kicked out of my apartment with a college degree while simultaneously being told I was overqualified for minimum wage jobs?

Riddle me this, if a high-achieving, uber-confident, college-educated
woman screams and loses her mind in the forest, but no one is around to hear her, does she still make a sound? I'd unequivocally say, yes. But after months of beating the pavement for a job both virtually and physically, it was time to concede.

The money I had so carefully stashed away for a rainy day had come to an end. What was wrong with me?

The moment had finally come. I had to call home to my mom and admit defeat.

I was a college graduate with real-world experience, but I STILL couldn't land a job. As I dialed my mother's number, and the phone rang, a warm flush of shame and embarrassment crawled up the back of my neck. Upon hearing my mother's greeting and nickname for me, "Hey Boot!" the guilt of her sacrifices for me to attend college overwhelmed me and I burst into tears.

I was a failure. I felt like a fraud. She set me up for success, but I couldn't make her proud. I felt like a burden, financially, emotionally, and soon to be physically because I was about to move home.

Though my dreams of being an independent adult shattered, in my broken gibberish, half-talking and half-crying guilt, my mother threw me a lifeline. She said, "Don't break your lease yet. You've got 30 days to make something happen, if you don't find something by then, we'll come up and move you home." As my tears slowly dissipated, a faint glimmer of hope appeared.

To be clear, 30 days was not a lot of time to find a job, especially since I'd spent the last several months looking for one, but it was better than nothing. And the definition of insanity is doing the same thing over and over again and expecting a different result. So, it was time to throw away everything I was "taught" and come up with a new game plan.

If I was going to succeed this time, I had to do things differently. I had to be creative and think outside the box to ensure that the red clay dirt road where I grew up did not become a permanent fixture in my future.

So, the question I asked myself before changed from, "What's wrong with me?" to "What am I doing wrong?" to "What's missing?".

And I'd liked to say, that this self-reflective process was super organized and routine, yet it was anything but easy. I tore everything down and everything apart to see if I could locate the problem. From resumes to interviews and more, nothing was safe.

I'd like to think that I did more personal development in those thirty days than I'd done in my four and a half years of college. I started asking the tough questions and really began sitting in silence waiting for the answer to be revealed. People say, you are never as close to God as when you need something, and whether that's right or wrong, that was certainly the case for me.

Questions I'd previously ignored before, we're suddenly taken seriously and entertained with an entirely different perspective.

- What did I want to be when I grew up?
    - Well, to be honest I don't know (Problem #1)
- Why haven't I found a job yet?
    - I really didn't want to be at the companies I applied to. (Problem #2).
- What was so bad with moving back home to Jackson, SC?
    - I was afraid to move home and get stuck in a rut, but more than anything else I was just embarrassed (Problem # 3).

The more questions that I asked myself and answered honestly, the clearer it became. I came to understand that it was less about the survival of the fittest, and more about where I fit best. With the 30-day ticking time bomb quickly approaching, it was time to make another phone call.

But this time instead of the shame of embarrassment I was able to call my mother with a swell of excitement and pride. I did it! Well kinda. I landed another internship. And while it was only a few months, essentially, I got another three-month extension. It wasn't the perfect scenario, but I was determined to make the best of it.

Instead of brooding about the unfairness of it all, I focused my energies on the task at hand: turning this short-term assignment into a permanent one. With a new mindset and a new plan, I buckled down, put on my big girl panties, and made it work. And my efforts were rewarded! A few weeks before the end of my internship I was offered a full-time opportunity that was actually related to my degree.

In a strange plot twist, I had to end my internship early so I could start working. Finally, a permanent and stable position I could really use as a starting point to launch my career. The salary was more than I'd ever expected, and I had all the benefits to match. It was like the stress of the last year disappeared overnight. The sleepless nights, the constant worry, the never-ending anxiety that wakes you up in the middle of the night, simply vanished.

I felt vindicated and knew that without a doubt absolutely NOTHING was wrong with me. It was more about what I was doing wrong in the job searching process. And that's why I'm sharing my journey because I know I'm not alone.

Chapter 3: Why I'm Sharing

During my unemployment I felt extremely isolated and alone. I felt like I was in this situation by myself and looking back I can easily see now I was depressed.

- Excessive weight gain in a short period of time.
- Losing interest in routine activities.
- Avoiding friends and family because just talking on the phone was just too much for me.

I was tired and ashamed.

It wasn't until I started sharing my journey years later with others that people started sharing their own stories about the difficulty of landing a career that didn't result in living paycheck-to-paycheck. The more honest I was about my own struggle, the more gut-wrenching stories people felt comfortable sharing. As a person of color, you can't hide the ugly truth about how hard it is to land a job and the helplessness you feel when you can't provide for yourself and your family.

Car repossessions, the feelings of inadequacy, deciding which bill is more important to pay this month, plummeting credit scores, credit collectors calling nonstop and harassing you, avoiding going to the doctor because it's so expensive, staying in relationships past its expiration date because they couldn't afford to leave financially. The list goes on and on.

I finally realized NOT sharing my story was more detrimental than anything else I could ever do. And I also came to the conclusion that people were comfortable confiding their deepest fears and some of their darkest shame with me, because they never had a safe space to do so without judgement. In essence, these individuals were looking for something that my mother had gifted me with so many years ago; a glimmer of hope.

If you made it to this page, trust me, it is not by accident you have made it this far. You came searching and seeking answers while wishing against your better judgement that a change could be found. The following pages of this book will reveal what you've been waiting for. Because finding your dream job and getting paid what you deserve is more than just resumes and interviews. It's really about your freedom. Let's begin.

Chapter 4: So, How Does This Really Work?

You are brilliant. You know more than you think and are more valued than you could have ever imagined. But the job-searching process can have you thinking and feeling the exact opposite.

Repeated email rejections from online applications, constantly interviewing, and showing up to networking events, with business cards in one hand and a glass of Moscato in the other gets old really fast. And if the thought of completing one more application makes you mentally exhausted then it's definitely time to take a break because you are experiencing what I call job fatigue. Job fatigue is when you are mentally and emotionally drained from the job search process.

For most people, looking for a job can feel like a full-time job. And there is only so much time before all of that extra work and effort catches up to you. If you land a job, most people feel like it's time well spent. But usually, most workers aren't that lucky. And the reason you aren't as successful in landing a job is because you are depending on luck and not strategy.

Essentially, you are leaving one of the biggest aspects of your life up to chance. Success will not come until you get serious and craft a plan that works for you.

Let's go back and examine how applying for a job at Mercedes-Benz, a job that was 600+ miles from my home, was part of a larger plan and strategy.

When I applied for a position at Mercedes-Benz, I was working in Human Resources as a Talent Acquisition Recruiter or as I was more affectionately called, the "happy career fair lady." I went to career fairs to share opportunities, I sat down with managers to understand what they were looking for in candidates, I also interviewed, hired, and even onboarded new hires and interns. My job was really cool, and

I loved the impact of it, but my mentor told me it was time to move on.

He said that in order for me to get the best role I needed to identify skills that were valuable and important to the company, not just to me. So, I researched and did my due diligence, and I discovered that compliance was a really hot topic in HR. Then a new problem revealed itself; I didn't have any experience in compliance.

Have you ever been there?

Found a job that you could probably do, but didn't have the "right" experience according to the job description? I was the happy career fair lady. A happy-go-lucky extrovert who loved people. How was I supposed to present myself as a serious analytical, data-driven problem solver with experience in policies, procedures, and auditing?

Simple, I asked for help. I knew I was in over my head and I also knew this wasn't my current mentor's area of expertise. I had to reach out to other trusted colleagues and family members for guidance and support. If anything, I learned from being unemployed before was that I couldn't isolate myself and retreat inward, I needed to step out.

Now let's be clear, this is easier said than done. But I didn't want to be labeled and get "stuck" in a recruiting role forever, so I had to take a leap of faith and figure it out, but I didn't do it blindly. I had to create a strategy. A roadmap of sorts to determine what are the three key factors I needed to know when selecting a new mentor.

I discovered in order for me to be successful with a new mentor I needed to know three particular things:

1. I needed to know what specific goal I wanted to achieve, and clearly communicate what I wanted from this specific mentoring relationship.
2. I had to make the decision and be okay with the fact that in order to find the right mentor for me, I may

have to spend some money and invest in myself to get the results that I really wanted.

3. I needed a time-limit for how long this relationship would last. I know Rome wasn't built in a day, but I needed results, and I knew this relationship couldn't last forever, to achieve this one particular goal.

Check out one of my brilliant clients Tyler Young and the results we were able to achieve together once she set a goal and decided she needed a mentor.

Case Study

Tyler Young

Hey everybody my name is Tyler Young and I am a writer and producer. I'm also a client of Ashley Dash and I'm here to tell you about all of the awesomeness that comes with being one of her clients. I believe she and I began consulting in 2013 and I have seen such tremendous change in my life since I brought her on my team.

I will say that I'm more confident than I was in 2013. I was at a point in my career where I was really burned out as a news producer at the time and I just wanted a change for myself. I wasn't sure what that change was going to be I just knew that I wanted to stay in television in some capacity but not in actual news broadcasting. So, I came to her and I was not happy. I was a Negative Nancy. I was Sad Susie. I don't think they're the same but whatever. At the end of the day I was truly a Debbie Downer and she listened to me. She heard me out. I just went to my meeting with her and I truly dumped off all of my problems, and her first response to me was- "What are you gonna do about it?"

I hadn't even thought that far. I was just so disgusted with my current work situation that all I could do was complain. And so she truly analyzed what was going on with me and she realized that part of my issue wasn't the *job, it wasn't the environment, it was truly me. I needed more for myself and I wasn't putting in the work Point Blank period, so she and I began to work on my resume.*

Okay, so what things did I needed to add to my resume meant I need to know what kind of job I'm looking for. And so I was like oh maybe I'll be a publicist, or maybe I'll go back to school and she's like "No, No, No! You're missing the point. You're still coming up with excuses for yourself. You want to be in TV don't just pick out random jobs that seem similar you need to truly pursue a career."

I got to a point where I realized she was right. I needed to do something about my situation and at a time my quick fix was for me to resign from my position. Yes, I left my full-time career to become a freelance career girl. I didn't know what exactly this was going to entail for my future, but I knew I had a career coach in my corner the entire time. I would call her all the time and she's always there to answer my call. She looked over my resume, she and I would do mock interviews, and she'd also help me with networking.

I would say networking was my biggest weakness at the time when she and I first began working with one another. I was not really good with staying in contact with people. I would literally get someone's business card, say "Yeah, we'll stay in contact," and six months later I would find that business card under my bed while I was cleaning up. And I'm like who is this person, I don't think I know who this is. I picked up this card by mistake and I'd truly throw it away.

So she really helped me build healthier professional relationships. That is one thing that she will always make sure that she works with you on is building a strong professional network. She is truly, truly big about making sure that you are consistent. I was consistently inconsistent.

I would be working really, really hard and I'd have this fire burning in me and then I'd get burned out on whatever project I was working on at the time. I'd get burned out and no lie she always called every time saying, "Tyler what's going on? You told me you're working on this, why are you not staying on top of this?" "Jeez you're right I need to get back on it," I'd say, so she is truly a cheerleader always in your corner she will not let you slack.

Also, I just want to say that I work with Oprah recently Oh-Prah, Mother Oprah. I met Oprah I believe two weeks ago oh my goodness so this goes from a girl crying about her life in 2013 not knowing where I was going to go to being in the same general vicinity as one of the greatest media moguls of our lifetime.

It's just absolutely phenomenal and I would like to say that Ashley Dash helped me to build myself up to that point. She always checks on me and any time she calls me I always have a blessing come through. So thank you Ashley Dash for helping me to network and build those relationships so that I am now able to build a successful career for myself.

Chapter 5: So, How Do I Get There?

I know what you're probably thinking, that's great for you and Tyler, but, how do I get there? How do I move forward in my prospective career? It's probably one of the questions I've gotten the most.

As I continued on in my career, people would often ask me, how'd you land your role there? And I'd naively say, "Oh, I just applied" or "Oh, I just spoke to so-and-so." Because in my mind it really was that simple and easy. But, what I failed to consider and share with those who asked, was all of the time and effort I spent reading, researching, and asking questions of my mentors to land the roles I was getting. I had truly found career freedom. That's why I was able to relocate, change roles, and make the money I had only dreamed about in the past. And career freedom is how Tyler was able to meet Oprah.

Having career freedom means, you can get the job you want, anytime you want. Which means you're not stuck with crazy coworkers, or a micromanaging boss. You can hit the road and say "deuces" to any work situation without feeling stuck. But in order to do this you have to be open to change and be flexible.

Flexibility is the key in making boss moves and boss money in your career. Flexibility can show up many different ways in your career. For me being flexible has meant:

- Relocation
    - Moving from SC to NJ
    - From NJ to Silicon Valley
    - From Silicon Valley to Southern California
    - And then back to SC
- Learning new skills that got boring very quickly
    - "Ahem" Human Resources Compliance
- Saying yes to unexpected projects- such as leading the HRIS integration for Performance Management at work

- Asking for help REPEATEDLY
- Stepping outside my comfort zone and volunteering for events at the Mercedes-Benz Diversity office that I didn't really understand

Flexibility and adaptability are the career currency that separate the folks who hate their jobs, from the people who LOVE their job AND get paid a lot of money to do it. As I always say, my clients come to me brilliant and Da'Ron Carpenter was no different. He'd been at his current job for several years, and enjoyed it, but he knew it was a time for a change.

But like so many other people in the workforce, he was applying and applying for jobs, but he just couldn't seem to make the move. It was like there was an invisible barrier in his way, that he just wasn't able to move beyond. He reached out to me, and I coached him using my step-by-step Career Branding Blueprint™ and emphasized the importance of being flexible. After making the decision to invest in himself, he got more than he could have ever imagined, like the opportunity to get paid more to do less work! See for yourself his results in his own words.

Case Study

Da'Ron Carpenter

I have benefited from working with Ashley in that when I decided it was time for me to take the next step up the ladder. I was quickly able to obtain a promotion within the United States Department of Agriculture from the position of Food Inspector to Consumer Safety Inspector.

What I liked best about working with Ashley was how simple she made the whole process. Her directions were clear, concise, and extremely easy to implement.

Working with Ashley felt natural and effortless because our conversations would just flow and I would be given different insights and direction that I had never considered before, but have proven to be incredibly beneficial to me. For example: I didn't want to move far from South Carolina so I was mostly searching for positions in Georgia, South Carolina, and North Carolina. Ashley Dash said that I should consider Virginia because she felt I could thrive there. I had never really considered Virginia before but I trusted her advice and begin applying to jobs in Virginia utilizing all the tools and techniques she taught me.

In less than two months I had been offered a job in Virginia, which I accepted and it has proven to be a fantastic move so far.

I have recommended Ashley Dash's services to close friends and relatives because I care about them and want them to be successful. And I know they can if they implement the tools and techniques within the program. I also have recommended the services to coworkers because I have seen people go for years attempting to be promoted with no success. A lot of them with similar or even more experience than I have.

Ashley's services are more than just about one job or one promotion but have given me life skills that I continue to implement over and over again in other work and business environments. I have mostly always had positive relationships with my coworkers and supervisors in the past, but there is a night and day difference between how I use to interact with them and how I now interact with them because of the "soft skills" I have learned to use.

The main thing I have learned from Ashley Dash's services is that it takes more than just experience and education to move up the ladder. You have to know how to present that experience and education in order to stand out among other applicants. And this program will get you to where you want to be in your career if followed.

Chapter 6: But, What If...?

Da'Ron's results were quick and fantastic, and you're probably thinking, how do I know if the blueprint will work for me? Fear is a very powerful emotion, and I don't think we talk about it enough. We're told to ignore fear or "just get over it", but does that really help?

I've learned from experience that fear is more than just a four-letter word. It really is the hundreds of questions that pop into your mind when you're making a major decision. It's the unpredictable nature in the unknown of the future. It's the "But?" that comes before every decision you make.

- But, what if it doesn't work?

- But, what if it doesn't work for ME?
- But, what if I don't think I can't afford it?
- But, what if someone changes their mind
- But, what if I don't get hired?
- But, what if I move and I don't like it?
- But, what if my family doesn't approve?
- But, what if I have to move?
- But, what if I don't like it?
- But, but, but, but, but…?

I could go on and on with all the questions, and it wouldn't help? Fear can oftentimes feel stronger than any story, fact, figure or rationale that I could ever provide. I went to this conference in

Atlanta, GA and I remember this facilitator describing fear as an emotional hijacking. I remember thinking "that's a bit of a harsh way to describe fear," but I've come to understand that she was exactly right. Fear not only makes you nervous physically, but it drains you of your drive and energy emotionally, and it robs you of your innate power and ability.

In order to keep your power, you have to be courageous. But courage doesn't mean that you are never afraid or will never experience fear again. It means, that with the fear, with the crazy feeling in the pit of your stomach you take the action anyhow, not always confident of the end-result, but just knowing that you at least had to try.

I'd like to share with you another client, Crystal Starkes. She's a Remarkable volunteer leader and youth development extraordinaire. She's brilliant, prepared, and terrified.

In one of our coaching sessions, she found herself unsure of her next steps. She wants the promotion, but a number of fears clouded her judgement. But the one thing that I know will change her life, and yours too, is realizing you have a choice. It really is that simple.

You can choose to take action, or you can let fear and inaction guide your life.

The choice is up to you. And I know there are risks, questions, and external factors that get in the way of your decision-making, but that's why you get a mentor. A proven step-by-step plan to guide you forward is the only way. Let's check out what Crystal had to say, in her own words once she got a mentor and a plan.

Case Study

Crystal Starkes

I owe my current position to Ashley Dash! She coached me in resume and cover letter writing to interview preparation and attire. I felt more confident when I walked into the door for my interview. Choosing Ashley Gary-Roper to assist me was one of the best decisions that I've ever made!

Chapter 7: So, What Now?

So, I'm definitely not a science major, but Newton's Third Law of Motion states, "For every action, there is an equal and opposite reaction." And if you're reading this book, there's a strong possibility that your actions have not provided the intended result of career freedom and job satisfaction just yet. I remember all too well the frustration caused in both my personal and professional life, all because I wasn't happy in my career.

I remember:

- Robbing Peter to pay Paul because I was barely making ends meet.

- Feeling guilty that I was bothering people asking for help.
- Feeling like a burden to my family and friends who had already done so much for me.
- Feeling lost like I wasn't fulfilling my God-ordained purpose in life.
- Feeling unhappy all the time, but not knowing why or how to fix it,
- Feeling like this was all there was to life: working, paying bills, and repeating a vicious cycle.
- I felt like I was merely existing but not REALLY living.
- Overlooking the disrespect I was experiencing at work, because I felt like I "NEEDED" a job to pay my bills.

- The multiple projects and promotions I was overlooked for because I wasn't the right "fit".
- The extra work I took on without being compensated for it.
- Being repeatedly rejected for jobs and not landing the interviews.
- Landing the interviews but always coming in second best.

And the list could go on and on. If only I had known sooner, that the issue wasn't money, or my job, or my crazy coworkers, or my boss, but the void that I was feeling came from my personal life. I was the captain of my destiny, I just didn't know it at the time.

I didn't know that people from small schools in South Carolina could land multiple job offers, and $100,000 jobs in 30 days or less. I didn't know that companies outside of the military offered to relocate you across the country and provided tens and thousands of dollars in sign-on bonuses just for being you. I didn't know that you could apply for jobs, and hear back in less than 24 hours because your skills were so highly coveted in fields outside of engineering and tech. All results I have gotten not just for myself, but for my clients.

I didn't know that having a branded resume was important, and a key asset that managers and supervisors could use as a tool to help them remember you during the hiring process. I thought that you had to attend Harvard, a top 10 business school, or at least a state-supported flagship university to get any respect in your career. None of these applied to my success.

I didn't know that getting a mentor and creating the right career brand was the key and made all the difference in the world. So that I could not only increase my confidence and make more money, but truly find freedom at work. If only I would have known sooner, I could have avoided all the heartache, stress, and worry. I could have avoided the frustration, disappointment, and guilt.

I could have saved more money, and already had a six or seven-figure investment portfolio, and multiple rental properties and other passive streams of income. But here's the secret, now YOU know. You now have all of the information, I didn't have many years ago. So the new question is, "What are you going to do about it?".

Chapter 8: How do I Get Unstuck and Find Career Freedom Today?

You can find your dream job and get paid more than you ever imagined. You're NOT stuck. Even though you may feel that way. You just need a guide and some help along the way.

So reading this book means ABSOLUTELY NOTHING, if you don't take the action steps to back it up. Below are three practical steps that you can do take right now to ensure your proven path to career freedom.

First, go to careercorneroffice.com/quiz and take the career personality quiz. It's super simple, it's super short, and you can learn more about what actions steps to take that will lead you towards career success today. Detail your results below for your reference now and for the future:

Record Results

Career Personality Type:

_____

Next, for those of you who need it, let's tackle a key branding asset in your career portfolio; your resume. Now, before you run screaming for the hills, I'm going to show you how you can revamp your resume in less than five minutes.

The 5-Minute Branded Resume Make-Over

Branded resumes have a framework regardless of industry. The Good to G.R.E.A.T. (G2G) resume philosophy teaches you how outline and describe your resume without spending loads of time banging your head against your keyboard. The quick and dirty version is below, but if you want the free PDF and resume checklist, you can join my list by heading over to http://careercorneroffice.com/resumechecklist.

Now for the Good to G.R.E.A.T resume strategy.

Your resume should show <u>Growth</u>: Brand your resume by using key industry words at the top of your summary of qualifications or business profile to give your resume a cohesive, growth-oriented feel. **90 seconds** of your makeover time will be spent here.

Make sure your resume is <u>Realistic</u>: Just don't lie! Know your strengths and weaknesses. If you don't fit a job description, save yourself some time by not saying that you do. This takes approximately **0 seconds** of your makeover time.

Your resume should be <u>Easy</u>. Style is just as important as content. You can download a free resume template in Microsoft Word or invest in a branded one with me. Trust me, it is worth the small investment of your time and energy to find a new format. Just go to www.careercorneroffice.com/rapidresum eresults to learn more. This will take up about **60 seconds** of your time.

Your resume should be <u>Appropriate</u>: The content on your resume should be customized for your industry. Head over to Google and type in your desired job title then select images. Get some ideas from the competition for your own resume. You will need only **90 seconds** to complete this task.

Finally, your resume should be <u>Timely</u>: Ensure that your resume ha the correct date ranges including month and year for your work experience. Unless you are applying for a leadership position, delete any positions that are 10+ years old. This includes graduation dates, if necessary. This will use your remaining **60 seconds** of time.

Now, that you have a branded resume, there's one more step that you need to take, and that's finding the right mentor. You are not an island, and whether you know it or not, you need accountability, you need a support system, and you need a team. So take some time right now answer these questions, so you can find your mentor.

What specific goal do I want to reach in my career? More money? A better work-life balance? Landing a promot on?

Write down your thoughts below.

_____

_____

_____

_____

_____

_____

_____

_____

How do I plan on getting there? And be really honest, right here. You've tried things in the past that didn't work, so what are you going to try different this time around? (Be prepared to share this information with your mentor in the future).

_____

_____

_____

_____

_____

_____

_____

_____

Am I worth the time and investment of finding the right mentor to pursue my future? (Answer: Abso-freaking-lutely!)

_____

_____

_____

_____

_____

_____

_____

_____

Now these steps, are only a first step as part of a larger strategy. But, it should give you enough relief right now, to move forward. Just take the very next step right in front of you. Because remember, any progress is still better than no progress at all.

Chapter 9: Can You Help Me?

The short answer to the "Can You Help Me?" question is absolutely! Why, yes I can. But the more important questions should be:

- Are you willing to take action?
- Are you willing to bet on you?
- Are you willing to do something totally different than you probably have ever done before?

If you answered yes to all three questions, I invite you to complete an application to work with me by going to workwithashleydash.com. You see, I have a step-by-step guide that I think will really help. It's part of a 60-day coaching mentorship with me that teaches you how to increase your confidence, make boss money, and find freedom at work.

It's called The Career Branding Blueprint™, and it teaches you how to Get on a Proven & Profitable Path so that you create a brand so strong that it speaks for itself, so you can live a life you LOVE! There are eight modules in the blueprint and they include:

- Module 1- Healing Work Hurt™: Learn how to deal with work blocks that keep you stuck from moving forward in my career and making the money you KNOW you deserve.

- Module 2- Trusting Yourself Again: Increase your confidence so you can trust yourself to navigate Corporate Politics seamlessly. Learn to forgive yourself for mistakes and experiences that prevent you from taking action and moving forward?

- Module 3- Focus Your Future: Get explicitly clear on what you want and why you want it for your CAREER and life. But not just for yourself, but for your family.

- Module 4- Network Your Niche: Begin building a SIX-FIGURE network so you can make your own power moves. Start Building Your

Bench so You Can Make Your do what you want, when you want.

- Module 5- Brand Like a Boss: Create a career brand so strong that it speaks for itself!

- Module 6- Confident Conversations: Learn the leadership communication strategies that SHOWCASE your genius and level the playing field.

- Module 7- Interview Like a S.T.A.R.: Learn the answers to the interview questions before the hiring manager even opens their mouth. Learn the mindset and strategy needed to make the best first impression, every single time.

- Module 8- Stack the Deck: ELIMINATE all the extra work during the hiring process and stack the deck so the ONLY logical answer is YES! I'll teach you how to jump on the Inside Track, to ensure You're Getting Paid What You Deserve.

The reason the blueprint is by application only is because it is NOT a fit for everyone. And that's completely okay! If you're not a fit, we'll find a program or even another mentor. I want to see you win.

I'm not here to convince you to do anything that does not benefit you. Doing so would be even more damaging than being stuck in a job you hate. My goal is to help, and sometimes, that means helping you on to someone else.

As I come to a close, I'd like to thank you for the time you spent with me to share my life and my life's work with you. It was truly an honor and a privilege. And as I always say, until next time,

-Loveyalaterbye

Ashley Dash
CAREER BRANDING EXPERT™

About the Author

Ashley Dash, Career Branding Expert™
and Creator of
www.CareerCornerOffice.com.

Speaker, Career Branding Expert™, and founder of CareerCornerOffice.com, Ashley Dash has been featured in *CareerBuilder, The Network Journal,* and *Internet Billboards.* She has also been a featured panelist for The National Urban League.

Ashley Dash teaches minority business professionals how to strategically brand themselves to land their dream job. Ashley knows what it's like to wake up morning after morning hitting the snooze button multiple times because she was dreading the work day. Not only was she unhappy, but she was definitely not getting paid enough to deal with the stress of it all.

Ashley went from being unhappy in a dead-end "job" to transforming her life and career with luxury car manufacturer Mercedes-Benz. This strategic move not only unlocked her earning potential with a $100K+ salary and huge signing bonus, but it also came with a corporate account, international travel—lifestyle perks beyond her wildest dreams.

Ashley Dash now leverages her nearly ten years of experience working with Fortune 500 companies into a PROVEN system that generates big results for her clients. Using her Career Branding Blueprint™ her clients have landed promotions in both public and private sectors and increased job satisfaction. Her niche: teaching her clients how to create careers and increase their work-life balance landing $100,000 salary offers in as little as 30 days.

Ashley has a Bachelor of Science in Business Administration from Winthrop University, a Master of Business Administration, and is pursuing a Doctorate of Strategic Leadership at Regent University.